A Chekhov Concert

Photograph by Michael Im

A Chekhov Concert

Duets and Arias

from the Plays of Anton Chekhov

Conceived and Composed by
Sharon Gans
and
Jordan Charney

Based on a Literal Translation from the Russian by Erika Warmbrunn

APPLAUSE
NEW YORK • LONDON

An Applause Original
A Chekhov Concert: Duets and Arias from the Plays of Anton Chekhov
Conceived and composed by Sharon Gans and Jordan Charney
Copyright © 1997 by Jordan Charney and Sharon Gans
ALL RIGHTS RESERVED.

The amateur and stock performance rights to this work are controlled exclusively by Applause Theatre Books, Inc., without whose permission in writing no performance of it may be given. Royalty arrangements and licenses must be secured well in advance of presentation. Royalty must be paid every time a play is performed whether or not it is presented for profit and whether or not admission is charged. A play is performed anytime it is read or acted before an audience. All inquiries concerning amateur, stock, and first class rights should be addressed to Applause Books, Licensing Division, 1841 Broadway, #1100, New York, NY, 10023, fax # (212) 765-7875.

No alterations, deletions or substitutions may be made in the work without the prior written consent of the publisher. No part of this work may be reproduced or transmitted in any form or by any means, electronic or mechanical, including photocopy, recording, videotape, film, or any information storage and retrieval system, without permission in writing from the publisher. On all programs, printing and advertising for the play this notice must appear: "Produced by special arrangement with Applause Theatre Books."

Due authorship credit must be given on all programs, printing and advertising for the play.

Library of Congress Cataloging-In-Publication Data
Gans, Sharon
    A Chekhov concert : duets and arias from the plays of Anton
  Chekhov / conceived and composed by Sharon Gans and Jordan Charney.
      p. cm.
    "An Applause original."
    ISBN 1-55783-273-0 (paper)
    1. Chekhov, Anton Pavlovich, 1860-1904--Adaptations. I. Charney,
Jordan. II. Title.
PS3557.A519C44 1997
812'.54--dc21   96-46840
                                                                               CIP

British Library Catalog in Publication Data
A catalogue record for this book is available from the British Library

APPLAUSE BOOKS	A&C BLACK
211 West 71st Street	Howard Road, Eaton Socon
New York, NY 10023	Huntington, Cambs PE19 3EZ
Phone (212) 496-7511	Phone 0171-242 0946
Fax: (212) 721-2856	Fax 0171-831 8478

Distributed in the U.K. and the European Union by A&C Black

Printed in Canada

The premier performance of *A Chekhov Concert* was at the Moscow Art Theatre, on May 20, 1991, starring Sharon Gans and Jordan Charney. This production marked the first occasion of Chekhov being performed in English by Americans on the Russian stage.

The authors wish to thank Anatoly Smelyansky, Dramaturg for the Moscow Art Theater, for his invaluable guidance.

ACT I

OVERTURE
Olga Knipper's final letter to A. Chekhov

BROTHERS AND SISTERS

The Seagull	1. Konstantin, Arkadina, Nina, Sorin
	2. Sorin, Arkadina
Uncle Vanya	Sonya, Vanya
Three Sisters	1. Olga, Andrey
	2. Irina
The Cherry Orchard	1. Ranyevskaya, Gayev
	2. Ranyevskaya, Gayev
	3. Firs

UNFULFILLED LIVES

The Seagull	1. Konstantin, Nina
	2. Medvedenko, Masha
"The Doctor Quartet"	Dr. Dorn, Dr. Astrov, Dr. Chebutykin, Dr. Chekhov
Uncle Vanya	Sonya, Dr. Astrov
Three Sisters	Andrey
The Cherry Orchard	1. Ranyevskaya
	2. Firs

REDEMPTION THROUGH WORK IN TIME

Three Sisters	Irina
The Seagull	Trigorin, Nina

The Cherry Orchard	Lopakhin
Uncle Vanya	Sonya, Vanya

ACT II

OBSESSIONS

The Seagull	Arkadina, Trigorin
Three Sisters	Tusenbach, Irina
The Cherry Orchard	Ranyevskaya, Gayev, Firs
Uncle Vanya	Vanya, Maria Vasilyevna
Three Sisters	Masha, Vershinin
The Cherry Orchard	1. Ranyevskaya 2. Trofimov

MOTHERS AND CHILDREN

The Seagull	Konstantin, Arkadina
Uncle Vanya	Maria Vasilyevna, Vanya
Three Sisters	Natasha, Andrey
The Cherry Orchard	1. Ranyevskaya, Trofimov 2. Lopakhin, Ranyevskaya

FINALE

Voices	Lopakhin, Nina, Arkadina, Dr. Dorn, Firs, Olga, Ranyevskaya

CODA

Olga Knipper's final letter to A. Chekhov (excerpt)

ACT I

The stage furniture is arranged as a turn of the century Russian living room and adjoining garden. Far stage right is a set of wicker garden furniture. Many of the interior pieces are draped in fabric. They include a chaise lounge, a small writing table and two chairs, a large comfort chair and ottoman, and, far stage left, an armchair and side table. The look is one of "shabby elegance." There are no walls, windows, or doors. Upstage of this setting is a large, hand-painted reproduction of a photograph of Chekhov cut into five panels forming the backdrop and side tormentors. Behind the drops is the back wall of the theater, or blacks.

As the house LIGHTS *go to half, we hear Beethoven's* Moonlight Sonata *fading up. Once the house is dark we hear the voice of* OLGA KNIPPER *reading from her last letter to Chekhov. The stage* LIGHTS *fade up to reveal* OLGA *reading at the UC table. The* MUSIC *slowly fades out.*

OVERTURE

OLGA KNIPPER: "September 11th. Darling, my dear, tender one, it's so long since I last talked to you! I've been nervous and restless, just the way you didn't want me to be. How I wish I could kneel in front of you now as I used to, rest my head on your chest and listen to your heart beating, while you stroked me tenderly — remember? Antonchik, where are you? Is it really possible you and I will never see each other again?! That cannot be. Our life was only just beginning, and suddenly everything's broken off, it's all over. How wonderfully you and I lived together! You kept saying that you never thought it possible to live so well as a married man. I had such blind faith that you and I still had such a long, long time ahead of us. Why just a few days before your death we talked and dreamed of the little baby girl that we were going to have. I have such pain in my soul that the child didn't remain. You and I talked so much about it. In November my little baby would already be two years old, but for the catastrophe. Why did it happen! A child would have outweighed everything for me, I feel sure. How you would have loved it! If only one could still dream about it! [*Pause.*] The theater, the theater...I don't know whether to love it or curse it...Oh, everything is so enticingly mixed up in this life! Now there is nothing in my life apart from the theater."

BROTHERS & SISTERS

[TRANSFORMATION. *(This indication in the script denotes the technique of transformation, in which the internal process is accented by the use of sound and movement, enhanced by the techniques of Michael Chekhov and the Open Theater.)*]

KONSTANTIN: We need new artistic forms!

OLGA KNIPPER: These three years have been a continuous struggle for me.

KONSTANTIN: New forms are needed, but if we don't get them, then better to have nothing at all.

OLGA KNIPPER: I lived in a constant state of self-reproach.

KONSTANTIN: I love my mother, I love her dearly.

OLGA KNIPPER: That's why I was so restless...so erratic...

KONSTANTIN: But she leads such a dissolute life.

OLGA KNIPPER: Couldn't settle down anywhere... make a nest for myself... a home...

KONSTANTIN: Totally obsessed with that novelist...

OLGA KNIPPER: It was as if I were always acting against my own conscience...

KONSTANTIN: Her name is constantly blown about in the papers... it exhausts me.

OLGA KNIPPER: And yet, who knows... had I given up the stage...

[TRANSFORMATION.]

ARKADINA: My precious son, when is it going to begin after all?

KONSTANTIN: In a minute, mother. I beg you to be patient.

ARKADINA: "O hamlet, speak no more:
Thou turn'st mine eyes into my very soul;
And there I see such black and grained spots
As will not leave their tinct.'

KONSTANTIN: "Nay, but to live
In the rank sweat of an enseamed bed
Stew'd in corruption, honeying and making love
Over the nasty sty.

[*A* HORN *sounds.*] Ladies and gentlemen... the beginning... I beg your attention... [*Pause.*] Please, I'm beginning. [*Knocks with a stick and speaks in a loud voice.*] Oh you honorable old shadows that hover in the night above this lake, lull us to sleep and let us dream of what will be in two thousand years!

ARKADINA: It is something decadent.

KONSTANTIN: Mama!

[KONSTANTIN *indicates to* NINA *to take center stage.*]

NINA: Men, lions, eagles, partridges, horned deer, geese, spiders, silent fish which dwell in the water, starfish, and that which one cannot see with one's eyes — in a word, all living things, all living things, all living things, have completed their doleful circle, died, extinguished... Thousands of centuries have gone since there has been a single living being on it, and that poor moon lights its lantern in vain...

KONSTANTIN: [*Whispers.*] In the meadow...

NINA: In the meadow the cry of cranes are heard no more, and in the lime groves the May Bugs are silent... Cold, cold, cold. Empty, empty, empty. Terror, terror, terror."

[TRANSFORMATION.]

[*Cross to chair.*]

ARKADINA: It smells of sulfur. Is that necessary?

KONSTANTIN: Yes.

ARKADINA: [*Laughs.*] Oh, I understand... Ah, yes... an effect.

KONSTANTIN: Mama!... Enough!... That's it... the play is finished! Curtain!

[TRANSFORMATION.]

ARKADINA: What's wrong with him?

SORIN: Dearest sister, mon petite soeur, Irina, one must not treat young pride this way.

ARKADINA: What do you mean... What did I say to him?

SORIN: You offended him.

ARKADINA: He himself told us it was a joke, so I related to his little piece as a joke.

SORIN: Nevertheless... dear sister...

ARKADINA: Now it turns out that he wrote a great work! Oh, for god's sake! So, he arranged this show, suffocated us with sulfur, not as a joke, but as a demonstration... to teach us, how to write, how to perform, how to act. Finally it's a bore. These constant sallies against me, these barbs... it would try the patience of a saint! He's a capricious, touchy child!

SORIN: He only wanted to make you happy.

ARKADINA: Is that so? But he didn't choose some usual kind of play, but forced us to listen to this decadent nonsense. For the sake of a joke I am as ready to listen to nonsense as anyone, but all we had here were pretensions to new forms, to a new era in art. But in my opinion, there are no new forms here, but simply bad character.

[TRANSFORMATION.]

ARKADINA: I have no money. I am an actress, not a banker.

[TRANSFORMATION.]

ARKADINA: ... Look after my son. Take care of him. Guard him. Admonish him... I must leave now, so I will never know why Konstantin shot himself. It seems to me, the main reason was jealousy, so the sooner I take Trigorin away from here, the better.

SORIN: [*Hums Ta-ra-ra Boom-bi-ya.*] It seems to me, it would be best if you could give him a little money. In the first place he needs to dress like a human being... [*Laughs.*] Yes, and it wouldn't hurt for him to run around a little...

to go abroad, for instance... that after all isn't so expensive...

ARKADINA: Anyway... Perhaps I can afford a suit, but to go abroad... No... in fact... at this time... I can't even afford a suit... I don't have money! [SORIN *laughs*.] I haven't! None!

SORIN: If I had money, please understand, I would give it to him myself, but I have nothing, not even a five-kopeck piece. My steward spends my whole pension on farming, cattle, and raising bees, and it is all a waste... the bees die, the cows die, and they never let me use the horses...

ARKADINA: I have no money. I am an actress, not a banker.

[TRANSFORMATION.]

SONYA: And you, Uncle Vanya, got drunk again with the doctor. Birds of a feather... Well, he's always been that way, but you — why? At your age it is altogether unbecoming...

VANYA: Age has nothing to do with it. When there is no real life, then you live on illusions... they're better than nothing.

SONYA: Our hay is all mown lying in the fields, it rains every day, everything is rotting, and you study illusions... You have completely abandoned the farm... I do all the work alone... I'm completely worn out and strained to the breaking point... Uncle... you have tears in your eyes...

VANYA: What tears? It's nothing... nonsense... You glanced at me just now exactly the way your poor late mother used to. My sweet... My sister... My sweet sister... where is she now? If she knew! Ah, if she only knew!

SONYA: What, Uncle? Knew what?

VANYA: It's so hard... not good... nothing... later... it doesn't matter... I'm going... [*Exits.*]

[TRANSFORMATION.]

OLGA: This is my brother, Andrey Sergeyich.

ANDREY: ... You have come to us as the new battery commander?

OLGA: Can you imagine, the commander comes from Moscow.

ANDREY: [*Pours a drink.*] Really? Congratulations! Well, now my sisters will give you no peace.

OLGA: Andrey is not only a scholar, he plays the violin... and he makes all kinds of little things with his hands. He's good at everything... Andrey, don't go! He has this little habit of disappearing all the time... Come back!

ANDREY: Well, enough! Enough... I didn't sleep all night and I am not quite myself, as they say... I read until four... then went to bed... but it was no use. I thought about this... I thought about that... [*Exits.*]

[TRANSFORMATION.]

IRINA: [*Alone.*] Oh, how our Andrey has become more shallow, there's no denying it... his spirit has left him... he's grown old living with that woman... The whole town gossips and laughs... but he alone... knows and sees nothing... all he does is sit in his room and play his violin... Oh!!! It's awful, awful, awful... I can't endure anymore... I can't. [*Weeping.*]

[TRANSFORMATION.]

RANYEVSKAYA: [*Laughing.*] The nursery!...My nursery, my sweet room, my wonderful room...I slept here as a little girl...And now I feel like a little girl again...

GAYEV: The train was two hours late...Can you imagine? What kind of management is that?

LUBOV ANDREYEVNA: Can this possibly be me sitting here? [*Laughs.*] I feel like jumping up and swinging my arms around. What if I'm dreaming?...I can't just sit... Oooh, I'm in such a state...I'll never be able to endure this joy...

[GAYEV *laughs.*]

LUBOV ANDREYEVNA: [*Cont'd.*] Laugh at me!...I'm so silly...My bookcase...my own bookcase...and my table...my sweet, little table.

GAYEV: And do you know, Lyuba, how old this bookcase is? Last week, I pulled out the lower drawer, I look, and there are numbers burnt into the wood. This bookcase was made precisely one hundred years ago. What do you say to that? We could have celebrated its jubilee! True, an inanimate object, but nevertheless, however you look at it, a bookcase. Yes...A real accomplishment... Dear, much respected bookcase, I hail your existence, *voici deja* more than one hundred years...for over a century you have served the glorious ideals of goodness and justice...your silent appeal to fruitful work has never flagged in the course of all those years, supporting in all the generations of our family, courage and belief in a better future and nurturing within us the ideals of goodness and social consciousness...

[*Pause.*]

RANYEVSKAYA: You are just the same as ever, Lenya.

a AYEV: Carom off the sides and into the right-hand corner! Slice in the center!

RANYEVSKAYA: Well, we've finished our coffee... Off to sleep...

[*Silence... Suddenly there is a distant sound, as if from the sky; the sound of a breaking string — dying away, sad.*]

[TRANSFORMATION.]

RANYEVSKAYA: Farewell, sweet house, dear old house of our fathers... Winter will pass, spring will come — and you won't be here — they'll pull you down... How much these walls have seen! It's as if I never saw what these walls were really like, and these ceilings... and now I look at them with such greed... with such tender love... We shall go and not even one soul shall remain.

GAYEV: My sister, my sister...

RANYEVSKAYA: Oh my sweet orchard, my dear and tender orchard, wonderful orchard!... My life, my youth, my happiness, Adieu... Farewell!... [*Pause.*] We are going! [*Exits.*]

FIRS: Locked. They're gone... Forgot about me... Well... Nothing... I'll just sit here a bit...

UNFULFILLED LIVES

[TRANSFORMATION.]

KONSTANTIN: I talked so much about new forms, but now I feel, that I am, little by little, slipping into the same old routine myself... It's horrible... Yes... and more and more I come to the conviction that it is not a matter of old forms or new forms, but that a person writes not thinking of any forms, but writes because it flows freely from his soul... What's that?... I can't see anyone... Someone ran down the stairs. [*Calls.*] Who's there?

[NINA *appears upstage wearing a hooded cape.*]

KONSTANTIN: [*Cont'd.*] Nina! Nina! Nina! It's you... you... I had a presentiment... my soul has been pining all day... Oh, my dear, my beloved... she's come! We shall not cry, we shall not.

NINA: Someone's here.

KONSTANTIN: No, no one's here.

NINA: Lock the doors — someone may come in.

KONSTANTIN: No one will come in.

NINA: I know Irina Nikolaevna is here... Lock the doors...

KONSTANTIN: This one has no lock... but I will block it with a chair. [*Moves armchair to block "door."*] Don't worry! No one will come in... there!

NINA: Let me look at you... It's warm here... it's good... This was the drawing room wasn't it?... Have I changed much?

KONSTANTIN: Yes... You've lost weight and your eyes have become bigger... Nina, it is somehow strange to see you... Why wouldn't you let me? Why didn't you come until now? I know you've been living here almost a week already... I've come to see you several times... I've been coming every day... And I stand under your window... like a beggar.

NINA: I was frightened that you'd hate me. Every night I dream that you look at me and don't recognize me. If only you knew what it's been like! Since the moment I arrived I have been coming here...walking 'round the lake...I've come by your house many times, but I couldn't bring myself to come in. Let's sit!!!

[*They sit together on the chaise.*]

NINA: [*Cont'd.*] We will sit and talk...talk and talk...it's good in here...it's warm, it's safe...Do you hear the wind? There's a passage in Turgenev somewhere: "Fortunate the man who on nights like this has a roof over his head and a warm corner." I'm the seagull...No that's not it!...[*Rubs her forehead.*] What am I talking about?...Ah, Turgenev..."And the lord help all homeless wanderers." [*She cries.*] It doesn't matter.

KONSTANTIN: Nina!!! You are crying again...Nina!

NINA: It's nothing...I feel relieved...I haven't cried in two whole years...then yesterday, late in the evening, I came to look at the garden...to see if our stage was still standing...and it is...even now...after all this time... I started to cry for the first time in two years, and I felt such a relief...and I became clearer in my soul...You see? I'm not crying now. So then, you've become a writer...You are a writer...and I am an actress...We have been pulled into the whirlpool of life...even us... I lived joyously like a child...I'd wake up in the morning and start singing; I loved you and dreamed of fame...and now, first thing tomorrow morning I go to Yeletz, in third class, with the peasants...and, in Yeletz the educated merchants will badger me with their courtesies...It's a coarse business...life.

KONSTANTIN: Why to Yeletz?

NINA: I took an engagement for the whole winter. It's time to go.

KONSTANTIN: Nina, I cursed you...I hated you...I tore up your letters and photographs, but every minute I realized my soul was bound to you forever...I do not have the power to stop loving you, Nina. Since I lost you and began to be published life has been unbearable for me, I can't live...I suffer...It's as if my youth was suddenly torn away, and that I've already lived on this earth for ninety years. I call out for you, I kiss the earth on which you walked...wherever I look your face stares back at me...that tender, gentle smile which lit up the best years of my life.

NINA: Why does he talk like that, why does he talk like that?

KONSTANTIN: I am all alone in the world...no one's affection warms me...I'm as cold as a dungeon, and, no matter what I write...it's all dry, stale and gloomy. Stay here, Nina, I beg you, or permit me to go with you!

[NINA *quickly puts up her hood.*]

KONSTANTIN: [*Cont'd.*] Nina, why? For God's sake, Nina...

NINA: My horses are standing by the gate. No...don't escort me, I'll get there myself...Give me some water...

KONSTANTIN: [*Gives her water.*] Where are you going now?

NINA: To town. [*Pause.*] Is Irina Nikolaevna here?

KONSTANTIN: Yes...On Thursday Uncle fell ill and we sent her a wire to come right away...

NINA: Why do you say that you kissed the earth on which I walked? I should be killed. I am so weary! If I could rest, rest...just rest! [*Sound and movement.*] I am the seagull...No, that's not it...I am the actress. Well yes! [*Listens, then runs and puts her ear to the "door."*] And he is here too...Of course...It doesn't matter...Of course he didn't believe in the theater...he laughed at my dreams, and slowly I stopped believing in them too and lost heart...And then there were the troubles of love... the jealousy...the constant fear for my little one...I became a petty thing, insignificant, my acting became meaningless...I didn't know how to stand on the stage...couldn't control my voice...I didn't know what to do with my hands...You don't understand how you feel when you know that you are acting badly...I am the seagull. No, that's not it...You shot a seagull, do you remember? Just by chance, one day, a man comes along and sees her and quite casually...destroys her... A subject for a short story. No, that's not it...It's not like that. [*Rubs forehead.*] What was I talking about? Ah yes, I was talking about the stage...Now, I am not like that...Now I am becoming a real actress...I act with enjoyment, with delight — ecstasy, I am drunk when I'm on the stage...intoxicated...and feel wonderful...and now while I've been living here, I've been walking and walking, thinking and thinking...and feel with every day my spiritual strength is growing...Kostya, I know now, I understand that in our work — in acting or writing — the main thing is not the glory, not the fame, not the things I used to dream about...but the ability to endure...bear your cross and have faith...believe...I believe now and for me it is not so painful...and when I think about my calling, I'm no longer afraid of life.

KONSTANTIN: You've found your path—you know your direction—while I'm still wandering in a chaos of broken dreams and images, almost completely useless. I believe in nothing...and I do not know what my calling is.

NINA: [*Listens.*] Shh...I'm going now. Farewell. When I become a great actress, come and see me act. Promise? But now...It's already late...I can barely stand...I'm worn out...I need to eat...

KONSTANTIN: Stay...I'll give you supper...

NINA: ...No, no...Don't escort me, I'll get there myself...My horses are close...So...She brought him with her?...Well, whatever...it's all the same... When you see Trigorin, don't tell him anything...I love him. I love him even more passionately than before...A subject for a short-story...I love him...I love him with all myself...I love him to despair...It was so fine before, Kostya...Remember? What a clear, warm, happy, pure life? What feelings—feelings like tender, elegant flowers...Remember? [*Recites.*] Men, lions, eagles, partridges, horned deer, geese, spiders, silent fish which dwell in the water, starfish, and that which one cannot see with one's eyes—in a word, all living things, all living things, all living things, have completed their doleful circle, died, extinguished...

[*Embraces* KONSTANTIN *impulsively and runs out.*]

KONSTANTIN: [*After a pause.*] No one must meet her in the garden and tell Mama...That would be bad...That could distress Mama...

[KONSTANTIN *goes to the table. He begins slowly tearing*

up his manuscripts and strewing them on the floor. He exits UL. After a beat, a GUNSHOT *is heard.*]

[TRANSFORMATION.]

MEDVEDENKO: Why do you always wear black?

MASHA: I am in mourning for my life. I am unhappy.

MEDVEDENKO: I long for you so much I cannot sit at home...every day I walk four miles here, and four miles back and am met with nothing but indifference. That's understandable. I have no money.

MASHA: Nonsense! Your love touches me, but I can't reciprocate, that's all...I can't. [*Offers him the snuff box.*] Here, have some...Help yourself.

MEDVEDENKO: I don't want any...But...you know, someone should write a play and put it on the stage and show how we teachers live. What a hard, hard life we have... hard life!...Your father won't let me have any horses.

[TRANSFORMATION.]

[DR. CHEKHOV *appears in a wheelchair pushed by* DORN. *They move DSC.*]

DORN: I have always found much that was good in my relationships with women...I think what they loved in me the most was my exceptional medical skills...If you will remember...ten to fifteen years ago I was the only really decent accoucheur in the province...not to mention the fact that I have always been a man of integrity.

CHEKHOV: [*Played by the actress. Her lines spoken with and between the other doctors.*] I think what they loved in me...

...not to mention the fact that I have always

ASTROV: I've become a different person these last ten years... Why? ...the reason being that I have been overworked... Since we first met I haven't had one day off. Is it surprising I've aged?

DORN: I am fifty-five years old.

CHEBUTYKIN: I'll soon be sixty—I'm an old man, a lonely nobody... an old man...

DORN: Eh! Well, then take some valerian drops... go to a spa... It is possible to go... it is possible not to go... There is nothing to understand... it is quite clear... tobacco and alcohol can deprive you of your individuality... you must take life seriously.

ASTROV: It drags you down, this life of ours... My feelings have somehow become blunted... I want nothing... need nothing... Love no one... I must admit that I am becoming a vulgar person ... See, I'm drunk too...

DORN: Would you like to take some valerian drops? Bicarbonate of soda? Quinine?

CHEBUTYKIN: The other day at the club they were talking about

---

been a man of integrity.
... Why? ... since we first met... is it surprising I've aged?

... a lonely nobody... an old man...
... Well, then, take some valerian drops... go to a spa... or not..

... Love no one...

... Would you like to take some valerian drops? Quinine?

Shakespeare and Voltaire. I've never read them. Not a word. I just put a look on my face as if I had. And the others did the same ...And off I went and started drinking...

ASTROV: Once a month I drink too much...and get drunk...like now...

DORN: To express dissatisfaction with life at sixty-two, is not very becoming.

ASTROV: In general I love life, but our Russian, philistine, narrow-minded life I have contempt for ...and despise it with all my soul ...And there is clearly nothing good about my own personal life...

You know, when you walk, on a dark night, through the woods and you can see a small light shining in the distance... then you tend to notice neither exhaustion nor darkness or the thorns of the branches that hit you in the face...but, for me, there is no little light shining in the distance.

DORN: I should go...

...our Russian, philistine, narrow-minded life ...despise it with all my soul...

...nor darkness ...but, for me, there is no little light shining in the distance.

ASTROV: I'm leaving today...

CHEBUTYKIN: I'm worn out...I don't want to talk anymore...

ASTROV: And I won't come here anymore...

CHEBUTYKIN: Anyhow, it's all the same...I'm tired...Let them have their little cry... [*Sings quietly.*] Ta-ra-ra-boombiya...Ta-ra-ra-boombiya...It doesn't matter does it? It doesn't matter...

DORN: Ta-ra-ra-boombiya...Ta-ra-ra-boombiya...

ASTROV: Ta-ra-ra-boombiya...It doesn't matter, does it? It doesn't matter...Ta-ra-ra-boombiya...I don't expect anything for myself...I don't have much care for others...it's been a long time since I've loved anyone.

...I'm leaving today...

...it's all the same...Tar-ra-ra-boombiya...It doesn't matter, does it?

...It doesn't matter, does it? It doesn't matter...

[TRANSFORMATION.]

SONYA: Tell me, Doctor...If I had a friend or younger sister and you found out that she...well...uh...let's assume that she was in love with you, say...how would you feel about that?

ASTROV: I don't know. Probably not at all, I imagine. I would try to make her understand, that I couldn't love her and that I have other things on my mind. In any event it's time to go if I'm going... and so, good-bye, my dear little one, or we'll be carrying on like this til dawn.

[*Shakes her hand and exits.*]

SONYA: [*Sound and movement.*] He's gone.

[*Pause.*]

SONYA: [*Alone.*] He didn't say anything to me... he didn't say anything... His heart and soul are still hidden from me... But then why do I feel so happy? [*Laughs with happiness.*] You are elegant, noble, you have such a gentle voice, I said to him... I hope it was all right to say that... The sound of his voice is so vibrant and comforting... I can feel it in the air all around me. But when I spoke to him about a younger sister he didn't understand. Oh, how terrible it is that I am not beautiful. How terrible! And I know that I'm not beautiful... I know... I know. Last Sunday, when they were leaving church, I heard some women talking about me, and one woman said to the other, "She's good... she's so generous... How unfortunate it is that she is not pretty."... Not pretty! [*Rises and crosses to sit on chaise lounge as* MASHA.]

[TRANSFORMATION.]

ANDREY: Oh where is it... where did my past go... when I was young, happy, intelligent, when I dreamed and had graceful thoughts, when my present and my future were illuminated with hope? Why is it that although we have barely begun to live we are already boring, gray, uninteresting, lazy, indifferent, useless, unhappy? Our town has been in existence for two hundred years already, in it are a hundred thousand inhabitants, and not one who did not resemble the others — not one zealot, neither in the past nor in the present, not one scientist, not one artist, no one the least bit outstanding who would excite envy or a passionate desire to imitate him. They only eat, drink, sleep then die... others are born and also eat, drink, sleep, and, then, in order not to expire from boredom, they vary their lives with nasty gossip, vodka, gambling, petty litigation; and the wives deceive their husbands and the husbands lie to themselves and pretend that they don't see anything, don't hear anything... and this irresistible, vulgar influence oppresses the children and the spark of god is extinguished in them [*Whoosh.*] and they become the same pitiable corpses resembling their fathers and mothers... The present is repulsive, but for all that when I think about the future, then how good it seems! It becomes so simple, with room to breathe, and in the distance a light begins to dawn, I see freedom, I see how my children and I will become free from emptiness, from kvass, from goose with cabbage, from dozing after lunch, from ignoble parasitic living off others... [*Seized by tender feeling.*] My sweet sisters, my magical, marvelous sisters! Masha, my sister... [*Rises and crosses to D bench and sits as* GAYEV.]

[TRANSFORMATION.]

RANYEVSKAYA: Oh, my sins... I've always squandered money like a madwoman, and I married a man who did nothing but amass debts. My husband died of champagne... and my misfortune was to fall in love with another man to whom I gave myself completely. It was just at that time — and this was my first punishment, it was like a great blow to my head, right in the river... my little boy drowned, and I went away, went abroad, went utterly away, went meaning never to return, never to see this river again... I shut my eyes, ran blindly—and he after me... pitilessly, callously. I bought a villa outside Menton, because he fell ill there, and for three years I knew no rest, by day or night. For three years he was an invalid—he drained my strength—my soul shriveled within me. And last year, when the villa was sold to pay my debts, I went to Paris, and there he robbed me openly, left me, and went off with another woman. I tried to poison myself... so stupid, so shameful... And suddenly I yearned for Russia, for my homeland, for my daughter... Lord, Lord have mercy! Forgive me my sins! Don't punish me anymore! [*Picks up a telegram.*] I got this today from Paris... He begs my forgiveness, implores me to return... [*Tears the telegram up.*]

[FIRS *goes to the door and tries the handle.*]

REDEMPTION THROUGH WORK IN TIME

[TRANSFORMATION.]

IRINA: There will come a time, when everyone will discover the reason for all this... for all this suffering, and what was buried from us will be buried no more... But for now it is necessary to live... necessary to work... only work! Tomorrow I will go away alone, I will teach in school and dedicate my whole life to those who might find it useful. Now it is autumn, soon it will be winter, and with winter will come the snows... and I will be working, I will be working, I will be working...

[TRANSFORMATION.]

[NINA *lies on wicker bench DSR.*]

TRIGORIN: ... You are talking about fame and happiness, and a kind of bright, fascinating life, but for me all these good words are like sugar plums... which I never eat... However, let's talk. We'll talk about my bright, wonderful life. Well, where shall we start? [*After a moment's thought.*] There exist on this planet *idees fixes*, certain ideas, of which man thinks of night and day... like the moon, for example... well... I have my moon. Night and day I am obsessed by one thought... I must write, I must write, I must write... Barely is one story finished, when for some reason I have to write another, then a third, after the third a fourth... I write ceaselessly, as if in a race on relay-horses, and I can't do otherwise. What's bright or wonderful about that, I ask you? What a rough life! Here I am with you, meanwhile, I'm worrying every second, remembering that an unfinished story is waiting for me. I see that cloud there, resembling a grand piano. I think: I will have to write, somewhere in a story, that a cloud resembling a piano floated by. Smells of heliotrope. I quickly make a mental note: sickly-sweet scent, widow's flower, use to describe summer evening. I catch myself and you on every phrase, on every word and hurry as soon as possible to lock all these phrases and words in my literary storeroom... they may be useful! When I'm through working, I will either go to the theater or go fishing; to rest, to forget myself, but no, a cannon ball is already beginning to spin inside my head—another image. My desk beckons me... and I must hurry again to write and write. And it is like that always and always... and I have no rest from myself, and I feel that I am devouring my own life... to make the honey for some stranger I'm tearing up my best flowers and stamping on their roots...Do you think I'm crazy?...While I write...it's quite pleasant...but as soon as it's barely off the press I can't stand it and see that it is not right, that it's a mistake, that it should not have been written at all and I feel vexed and worthless...However, as far as the public goes: "Yes, it's talented...it's interesting...Talented...but far from Tolstoy," or: "A wonderful work, but Turgenev's *Fathers and Sons* is better." And so on until I'm laid in my grave, everything will be only talented and interesting, talented and interesting—nothing more, and after I'm dead, acquaintances, walking by my grave will say: "Here lies Trigorin. He was a good writer, but he wasn't as good as Turgenev."...Success? I've never pleased myself. I don't love myself as a writer. Worst of all is that I go about in some sort of haze and often don't understand what I write. I love this lake, the trees that are here, the sky; I feel nature, it awakens in me a passion, an insurmountable need to write. But, in all fairness, I am not simply a landscape-ist...but also a citizen. I love the motherland, its citizens, I feel that as a writer, I have a responsibility to talk about the people, about their painful past and present...about their future, to talk about science, about the rights of man and so forth and so on...and I actually do talk about everything, but hurriedly, pressured on all sides, they get mad, I try escape by darting from side to side like a fox hunted down by dogs...I see that life and science keep going forward and forward, and I am left behind, like a peasant arriving too late for the train and ultimately I feel that I AM able to write only about landscapes, and in all the rest I am insincere...false to the marrow of my bones... And what do we have here? A seagull...Beautiful bird... I really don't much want to leave... Subject for a short story... A young girl living on the shore of a lake since she was a child, loves the lake like a seagull... and like a seagull she is happy and free... But, accidentally, a man comes along, sees her, and from idleness... destroys her... like the seagull here...

NINA: [*Sound and movement of "seagull."*] I am the seagull... No... That's not it... I am the actress. Yes. [*She crosses DS to sit as* RANYEVSKAYA.]

[TRANSFORMATION.]

LOPAKHIN: I bought it! Wait... please be so kind, ladies and gentlemen, my head is spinning... I can hardly speak. We came to the auction and there is Deriganov. Leonid Andreych had only fifteen thousand, and Deriganov, on top of the mortgage, immediately offered thirty. I see how things are going and so I take him on... I offer forty. He goes to forty-five... me... fifty-five. He keeps increasing by fives... me... by tens. Well, it closed at last. On top of the mortgage I offered ninety... and there it stopped. The cherry orchard is now mine! Mine! My God... Lord... the cherry orchard is mine! Tell me that I am drunk... that I'm not in my right mind, that I am NOT imagining all this. Don't laugh at me! If my father and grandfather would get up from their graves and look at all that has happened... how their Yermolai, beaten, ignorant Yermolai, who ran around barefoot in the winter... how this same Yermolai bought the estate that compares with no other in the world... The estate where grandfather and father were slaves, where they were not even allowed into the kitchen. I am sleeping... It only appears to be happening... it is simply the fruits of my imagination... the darkness of the unknown... [*Picks up the keys.*] She flung down the keys, she wants to show me she's no longer mistress here... [*Jingles the keys.*] Well, it doesn't matter... Hey, musicians, play, I wish to listen to music! Everyone come and watch Yermolai Lopakhin take his ax to the cherry orchard!... Watch the trees fall to the ground! We will build cabins, little summer houses, and the grandchildren and great-grandchildren will see a new life here. Music, play! Music!

[RANYEVSKAYA *has sunk down on to a chair.*]

LOPAKHIN: [*Cont'd.*] Why, why didn't you listen to me? My poor dear precious, you can't bring back the past. Oh, if only it were done. Oh, if only we could change our absurd, unhappy life... I bought it. The cherry orchard is mine! Mine!

[TRANSFORMATION.]

SONYA: [*Sound and movement.*] He's gone.

VANYA: [*At the abacus.*] ... another 20 pounds of lean butter... buckwheat... in total, 15... 25... I am so miserable, my sweet child. It is so hard for me. If only you knew how hard it was.

SONYA: But there is nothing to be done... it is necessary to go on living! [*Pause.*] What else to do, it is necessary to live! And we will live, Uncle Vanya, we will. We will live through an endless series of long days and nights, we will patiently bear the trials fate sends us; we will labor for others from now into our old age, and we will know no respite; and when our time comes we shall die humbly; and there, beyond the grave, we will say that we have suffered and wept, that our lives have known bitterness; and God will be moved to pity; and you and I, Uncle, dear Uncle, will see a life of light and beauty and grace; and we will rejoice; and we will look back on our unhappiness with tenderness, with a smile — and we will rest. I have faith, Uncle... I have a passionate faith... We shall rest! We shall rest! We shall hear the angels; we shall see all Heaven lit with radiance; we shall see all earthly evil, all our sufferings, drowned in the mercy which will fill the whole world, and our life will be peaceful, gentle and sweet as a caress. I have faith, I have faith... Poor, poor Uncle Vanya, you are crying... Your life has been without happiness, but just wait Uncle Vanya, wait ! we shall rest... we shall rest! we shall rest!

END OF ACT I

ACT II

OBSESSIONS

ARKADINA: Soon they will bring the horses... You are all packed, *j'espere*?

TRIGORIN: [*Impatiently.*] Yes, yes... Let's stay for one more day! Let's stay!

ARKADINA: My sweet, I know what holds you here... Pull yourself together... you're a little drunk... sober up.

TRIGORIN: Then, you become sober too... sober-minded and reasonable... I beg you, look at all this like a true friend. You are capable of sacrifice... Be my friend... set me free...

ARKADINA: Are you as enraptured as all that?

TRIGORIN: I am irresistibly drawn to her!... this may be exactly what I need.

ARKADINA: The love of a provincial girl? Oh, how little you know yourself!

TRIGORIN: Sometimes people walk in their sleep... I feel like that now... I'm talking to you but I am asleep and dreaming of her... Sweet and wonderful dreams... set me free.

ARKADINA: No, no... I'm an ordinary woman like everyone else... you can't talk to me like this... Don't tease me, Boris... it's terrifying.

TRIGORIN: If you chose... you could be extraordinary. Young love... charming, delightful, lovely, poetic... carrying me away to a world of daydreams... nothing else can give me such happiness! I've never experienced this kind of love before... There was no time when I was starting out in life... I was too busy pushing my way into editorial offices... and grappling with need... Now at last it is here, this kind of love calling at me like a siren... it would make no sense to ignore it.

ARKADINA: You're crazy.

TRIGORIN: Then let me go..

ARKADINA: You are all out to get me today.

TRIGORIN: She refuses to understand! Doesn't want to understand!

ARKADINA: Is it possible I am already so old and ugly that you can shamefully talk to me about other women? Oh, you have lost your mind! My wonderful man, my marvelous man... the final chapter of my life! My delight, my pride, my bliss... If you deserted me even for an hour, I could never endure it... I would lose my mind... my astounding man, my splendid man, my lord and master.

TRIGORIN: Someone could come in.

ARKADINA: They are welcome to... There is no shame in my love for you... My jewel, my despairing and desperate treasure... you go on raving like a madman, but I don't want you to and I won't let you go... You are mine... mine... this forehead is mine, these eyes are mine and this wonderful velvet hair is mine. All of you is mine. You are so gifted, so bright, the best of contemporary writers, Russia's only salvation. You have so much sincerity, clarity, vigor, and a robust sense of humor. With a single stroke of your pen you are able to communicate the essential nature of a person or a landscape so that they seem alive. Oh, it is impossible to read you without consuming ecstasy. Do you think this is empty praise? Mere flattery? Just look deep in my eyes...deep. Is that a liar you see in there? Only I can absolutely value you, only I tell you the truth, my dear and marvelous magician. You will leave with me...yes? You won't desert me?

TRIGORIN: Oh—God—I have no will of my own...I never have had. Spineless, manipulated, endlessly submissive—can this possibly really please a woman? Take me, lead me away—just stay by my side every moment.

ARKADINA: Now he is mine. [*Easily, as if nothing had happened.*] Of course, you can stay if you wish. I'll go myself and you come later...in a week or so. No reason for you to rush, really, is there?

TRIGORIN: No, we'll go together.

ARKADINA: As you wish...Together then...together.

[TRANSFORMATION.]

TUSENBACH: Irina, my love, I'll be back very soon.

IRINA: Nikolai, where are you going?

TUSENBACH: I have to go to town, to...say good-bye to some comrades.

IRINA: I don't believe you...you seem so distracted today...Why? [*Pause.*] What happened near the theater yesterday?

TUSENBACH: In an hour I shall return and again be with you...I've loved you for five years now, and I still can't get used to it. You seem more beautiful every day. What lovely hair! What eyes! Tomorrow I'll take you away from here, we'll work, we'll be happy, all my dreams will come true. There's only one thing: you don't love me!

IRINA: That is not within my power! I'll be your wife. Faithful and obedient. But it isn't love, I can't help it! I've never been in love. I dreamt of love for so long, day and night, but my heart is like a precious grand piano, which is locked, and the key lost. You do look worried.

TUSENBACH: I had no sleep last night. In my life there is nothing so terrible that could frighten me so much... it's only that lost key that torments my soul and won't let me sleep... Tell me something... [*Pause.*] Tell me...

IRINA: What? Tell what? What?

TUSENBACH: Anything.

IRINA: Enough! Enough!

[*Pause.*]

TUSENBACH: It is amazing how sometimes trivialities can acquire a significance in one's life, for no obvious reason. You still laugh at them and consider them nonsense, but don't have the strength within you to stop. Oh, well, let's not talk about that! I am happy. I am looking at these spruces, maples, and birches, as if it were for the first time in my life... and everything seems to be staring back at me... waiting with curiosity... What beautiful trees, and, in essence, what a beautiful life should surround them!... *Il faut aller*... time to go... There is a tree, withered and dried out, yet still able to sway in the wind with the others... I feel that is true for me as well... that if I die I will still take part in life one way or another. Farewell, my dearest... those papers you gave me are on my desk, in my room, under the calendar.

IRINA: I'm coming with you.

TUSENBACH: [*A gesture of "No!"*] Irina!

IRINA: What?

TUSENBACH: [*Not knowing what to say.*] I've had no coffee today... Would you ask someone to make me some?

[TRANSFORMATION.]

[*Sound of string breaking.*]

RANYEVSKAYA: What's that?

GAYEV: Perhaps some bird... maybe a heron.

RANYEVSKAYA: I don't know why but it fills me with dread.

[TRANSFORMATION.]

FIRS: Before the misfortune it was the same thing... the owl cried and the samovar hummed incessantly.

GAYEV: Before what misfortune?

FIRS: Before liberation.

[TRANSFORMATION.]

VANYA: Wait... You are selling the estate, outstanding, what an absurd idea. And where do you mean for me and my old mother and Sonya here to go? Up to now I naively supposed that we were not living under Turkish law, and that the estate had passed from my sister to Sonya... Now listen. This estate would not have been bought if I had not refused my inheritance on behalf of my sister, who I loved passionately. Moreover, I worked for ten years, like an ox, and paid off the whole debt...

The estate is free of debt and in perfect order thanks only to my own labors... Twenty-five years I managed this estate... worked, and sent you money, like the most conscientious steward and in all that time you never once offered me a word of thanks... For twenty-five years I have sat like a mole in the dark, shut up between these four walls with this mother of mine... All our thoughts and feelings belonged to you alone. During the day we talked about you, about your works, were proud of you, pronounced your name with reverence; the nights we spoiled reading magazines and books which I now deeply despise and hold in contempt... But my eyes are finally open! I see everything! You write about art, but understand nothing about art! You destroyed my life! I've had no life! No life! You are responsible for my having wasted the best years of my life! You are my eternal enemy! A lost life! I have talent, intelligence, courage. If I had lived like a regular person I could have been a Schopenhauer, a Dostoyevsky... I'm babbling like an idiot! I am going crazy... Mother, I am in despair! Mother!

MARIA VASILYEVNA: [*Sternly.*] Obey! Do as Alexander tells you!

VANYA: Mother! What should I do? No! Don't! It's not necessary to speak! I know what I have to do. You will not soon forget me! [*He exits quickly and returns with a revolver. He fires.*]... Bang! [*Pause.*] I didn't hit him? Failure again?! Ah, to hell with it... to hell with it... to hell with it... the devil take it...

[TRANSFORMATION.]

MASHA: I don't know. I don't know. Habit may have a lot to do with it, of course. After Father died, it took us a long time to get used to not having orderlies in the house. But habit aside, I think I can say it in all fairness... I don't know, maybe it's different elsewhere, but in this town the most decent, most honorable, most well-bred people are the military.

VERSHININ: I'm thirsty. I'd love some tea.

MASHA: They'll be serving it very shortly. I was married when I was only eighteen years old, and I was scared of my husband, because he was a teacher and I then had just finished school. Then he seemed terribly educated, intelligent, and important. Unfortunately, now it is not like that.

VERSHININ: Ah... Yes.

MASHA: It's not my husband I'm talking about... I'm quite used to him... but among the civilians in general there are so many people who are vulgar and coarse and uneducated... coarseness upsets me... it pains me... I suffer when I see a person who is not gentle, not kind, not gracious... when I'm among my husband's teaching comrades... I simply suffer.

VERSHININ: And to me it seems all the same... be they civilian or military, they are equally uninteresting, at least in this town... Yes... all the same! If one listens to a local intellectual, civilian or military, then you find someone worried to death about his wife, worried to death about his house, worried to death about his estate, worried to death about his horses. A characteristic of a Russian person is his exalted thinking, so then tell me why, when it comes to his living, does he fall so short? Why?

MASHA: Ah, yes... why?

VERSHININ: Why is he worried to death about his children... about his wife? And, conversely why are his wife and children worried to death about him?

MASHA: You are not yourself today, at all...

VERSHININ: Perhaps. I didn't eat lunch today... didn't eat anything since morning. One of my girls isn't feeling well, and when my daughters are sick, panic seizes me, my conscience torments me, that they have such a mother. Oh, if you could have only seen her today! What a dreadful person! We started to quarrel at seven o'clock in the morning and at nine I slammed the door and left. [*Pause.*] I never talk about this, never... Only to you... Strange, I complain only to you. Please don't be upset with me... Except for you I have no one... I'm alone... I have no one... no one.

[*Pause.*]

MASHA: What a noise in the stove! You know, just before father died there was howling in the chimney. There, just like that.

VERSHININ: So, you are superstitious...

MASHA: Yes.

VERSHININ: How strange... You are a magnificent and marvelous woman. Splendid and magical! It's dark in here, but I can still see the brightness of your eyes.

MASHA: It's lighter over here.

VERSHININ: I love you, I love you, I love you. I love your eyes... the way you move... I even dream about it... you splendid, magical woman!

MASHA: [*Laughing quietly.*] When you say things like that... for some reason it makes me laugh... although it frightens me. Don't say it again... I beg you...

[*Her voice drops.*] Or do... it's all the same to me. It's all the same. [*About to kiss.*] Someone's coming... talk about something else...

[*He moves DSR and listens as* TROFIMOV.]

[TRANSFORMATION.]

RANYEVSKAYA: I am so wretched today, you can't imagine! It seems so loud here... my heart jumps at every sound. I tremble all over, but I can't shut myself up; I can't bear the silence when I'm alone... [*Picking up the telegram.*] This is from Paris... a telegram... I get them every day... one came yesterday, another today. That savage is ill again; he's in a bad way... He asks me to forgive him, he begs me to come; and I really ought to go to Paris and be with him... What am I to do? What am I to do? He's sick, alone, and unhappy. Who is to look after him? Who is to keep him from doing stupid things? Who is to give him his medicine when it's time? After all, why should I be ashamed to say it? I love him, that's plain. I love him, I love him... My love is a stone tied round my neck; it's dragging me down to the depths; but I love my stone... and cannot live without it... Don't think badly of me... Don't say anything! Don't say anything!!!

[TRANSFORMATION.]

TROFIMOV: Humanity moves forward, developing its strengths. All that is now inaccessible, will some day become close and available. For the time being it is necessary for us to work and to use all our strength to help those seeking the truth. Here in Russia very few are working yet. The vast majority of that intelligentsia which I know is looking for nothing, is doing nothing and is not yet capable of real work... they philosophize. Meanwhile, in plain view, the workers are eating garbage and sleeping without bedding, thirty or forty in one room — everywhere bugs, smells, mildew, and moral decay... And, apparently, all these good discussions we have are only in order to deflect our attention as well as everyone else's. Show me where are our nurseries, that are talked about so much and often, where are the libraries? They are only written about in novels, in fact they don't exist at all. There is only dust and grime, trivialities, and inhuman behavior... I do not love their serious expressions... I am afraid of those serious discussions... Silence would be more valuable! ... We have lagged behind at least two hundred years... We don't have anything at all... no specific relation to the past. We only philosophize, complain about idleness, or drink vodka. And yet it is all so clear that to begin to live in the present it is necessary first to atone for our past — finish with it once and for all — and it is only possible to atone for it through suffering... through extraordinary and exceptional, never-ending labor. Understand this!!! ... Here it is, fulfillment, here it comes... marching nearer and nearer, I already hear the sound of the feet. And if we will not know it... if we will not recognize it... what difference does it make? Others will!!!!

[*They stamp their feet in unison.*]

MOTHERS & CHILDREN

[TRANSFORMATION.]

KONSTANTIN: Change my bandage, Mama. You do it so well.

ARKADINA: Sit down. [*Takes the bandage off his head.*] It's like you're wearing a turban. Yesterday a visitor in the kitchen asked what nationality you were. Ah, you're almost all healed. Only the slightest trace remains. [*Kisses him on the head.*] Kostya, there won't be any more click-click while I'm gone, will there?

KONSTANTIN: No, Mama. That was a fleeting moment of insane desperation, when I couldn't control myself. It will not repeat itself. You have such healing hands. I remember, long ago, when you were still working on the stage of the State Theater — and I was quite young — there was a fight in our yard and the laundress living in the building was severely beaten. Remember? She had been knocked senseless... when they finally got her to her feet... you went to see her repeatedly... brought her medicine, gave her children baths in the tub... You really don't remember?

ARKADINA: No. [*Begins to put a new bandage on.*]

KONSTANTIN: Two ballerinas also lived in the building... They would come and drink coffee with you...

ARKADINA: I remember that.

KONSTANTIN: I remember they were extremely religious. [*Pause.*] These last few days I've loved you as tenderly and absolutely as when I was a child. Other than you, I've no one left. But why, why do you allow yourself to be influenced by that man?

ARKADINA: You just don't understand him, Konstantin. He is a man of the noblest character.

KONSTANTIN: However when he heard that I was challenging him to a duel, his nobility didn't get in the way... He's leaving. Fleeing shamelessly.

ARKADINA: What nonsense! I asked him to leave.

KONSTANTIN: Most noble character! Here you and I are almost fighting because of him, and he is somewhere in the drawing-room or garden laughing at us... improving Nina, trying desperately to persuade her that he's a genius.

ARKADINA: You delight in being unpleasant to me. I respect that man and beseech you not to say bad things about him to my face.

KONSTANTIN: But I don't respect him. You would like it if I, too, considered him a genius, but forgive me, I cannot lie, his work sickens me.

ARKADINA: That is pure and simple jealousy. When someone has pretensions and no talent, they are reduced to disparaging those who do have talent. It must give you great consolation.

KONSTANTIN: Talent! I am more talented than all of you put together. [*Tears the bandage off his head.*] You and your friends are all hopelessly steeped in convention... but because of your high positions, you consider legitimate and real only what you yourselves are doing. Everything else you stifle and suppress. I don't recognize you... I don't recognize him!

ARKADINA: You decadent!

KONSTANTIN: Go! Go off to your precious theater and keep acting in those pathetic second-rate plays.

ARKADINA: I have never acted in such plays. Stop badgering me! You aren't capable of writing even a pitiful vaudeville sketch... You Kiev bourgeois... you shopkeeper... parasite!

KONSTANTIN: Miser!

ARKADINA: You beggar! You nobody! Don't cry. You don't need to cry. It's not necessary. My sweet child, I'm sorry. Forgive your sinful mother. Forgive this unhappy woman.

KONSTANTIN: If you only knew! I have lost everything. She doesn't love me... and I can no longer write... all my hopes have vanished... are lost.

ARKADINA: Don't be despondent. Everything will turn out all right. Soon he will leave... soon she will love you again. Everything will be fine. See, we have already made up...

KONSTANTIN: Yes, Mama.

ARKADINA: Make up with him too. Duels aren't necessary. Not necessary, after all?

KONSTANTIN: All right. Only, Mama, please, I don't want to see him. It is hard for me... I don't have the strength. There... I'm going out... the doctor will do the bandage... [*He exits.*]

[TRANSFORMATION.]

[VANYA *enters.*]

MARIA VASILYEVNA: This is awful...

VANYA: Nothing is awful. Drink you tea, Maman.

MARIA VASILYEVNA: But I want to talk!

VANYA: But we have been talking... for fifty years... talking and reading brochures... It's time we finished all that.

MARIA VASILYEVNA: For some reason you find it unpleasant to listen when I talk. I'm sorry, Jean, but you have changed so much in the past year, that I don't recognize you. You were a man of definite convictions, a bright personality.

VANYA: Oh yes indeed! I was a bright individual who illuminated nothing... [*Pause.*] You mustn't say such hateful things... I am forty-seven years old. I can't sleep at night. I'm so full of rage and resentment at having wasted my time so stupidly. I could have been anything, had everything, and now I can't; because of my age; I'm too old...

MARIA VASILYEVNA: It is as if you are blaming your earlier convictions for something. But they are not to blame... you are!!!

[TRANSFORMATION.]

NATASHA: Eight fifteen...? I'm worried. Our Bobik isn't well, the poor sweet. Why is he so cold? Yesterday he had a fever, and today he's cold. I'm worried.

ANDREY: The boy is fine, Natasha.

NATASHA: All the same it would be better if he were too eat lightly. I worry about him so much... And I heard that the mummers will be here tonight at ten o'clock... This morning he woke up and looked at me and smiled... He recognized me!!! "Bobik, hello!" I said to him. " Hello, my sweet!" And he laughed. Children understand, understand perfectly. So, that means, Andrusha, I will tell them that the mummers should not be allowed to come in.

ANDREY: That should be left to my sisters... After all, they manage the house.

NATASHA: They also manage it... I will tell them... They are good... Bobik is cold. I worry that his room is too cold for him. We should put him in a different room until the weather's warmer. Irina's room would do... it's perfect for a baby: dry, and sunny all day. I'm afraid you'll have to tell her... for now she can share with Olga... it doesn't matter... after all she's not home during the day, she only spends the nights here. [*Pause.*] Andrushka, why don't you say anything?

ANDREY: I'm thinking. Anyway, what is there to say?

[TRANSFORMATION.]

RANYEVSKAYA: My Grisha... my boy... Grisha... my son... My boy was lost... drowned... right in the river there... my little boy died. Why? Why, my friend?. Anya is sleeping there, and I am talking so loudly, making noise... What is it, Petya? Why have you grown so ugly? Why have you aged so?

TROFIMOV: A peasant woman in the train called me a shabby-looking gentleman.

RANYEVSKAYA: You were just a boy before, a pleasant-looking student, but now, you're balding, you wear thick glasses... Is it possible you're still a student?

TROFIMOV: I seem destined to be an eternal student.

RANYEVSKAYA: Well, go, get some sleep...And you've aged as well, Leonid.

[TRANSFORMATION.]

LOPAKHIN: I have to go to Kharkov...That's where I'm spending the winter.

RANYEVSKAYA: I am leaving with two troubles remaining. The first is sick Firs. Let's wait another five minutes... My second concern is Varya. [*Pause... to* LOPAKHIN.] You know this very well, Yermolai; I dreamed of giving her away in marriage to you...She loves you—you like her—and I simply do not understand why you try to avoid each other. I just don't understand! I don't understand!

LOPAKHIN: I admit, I too, do not understand. Everything is strange somehow...If there is still time, then I'm ready even now. Let's get it over with—and *basta*—but right now, because without your presence I will never propose.

RANYEVSKAYA: Excellent...After all only one minute is necessary. I will call her right now.

LOPAKHIN: Conveniently enough there is champagne... Hmm! Empty! Someone's been boozing it up...

RANYEVSKAYA: Wonderful. We will go out. I will call her. Varya, leave everything, come here. Come! [*Exits.*]

[*During the "Finale" section the echoes of some "Concert" characters are heard.*]

FINALE

LOPAKHIN: Kharkov...all winter. I've just been hanging

around here with all of you wearing myself out by doing nothing, I can't do without work, don't know what to do with my hands; they just hang down strangely, as if they were someone else's... When I work for long periods of time, which I can do without tiring, then thinking comes easier, and it seems as if I know why I exist... But how many people are there in Russia whose reason for existence is unknown to them?

[TRANSFORMATION.]

NINA: ...Kostya, I know now, I understand that in our work—in acting or writing—the main thing is not the glory not the fame, not the things I used to dream about... but the ability to endure... bear your cross and have faith... believe... I believe now and for me it is not so painful... and when I think about my calling, I'm no longer afraid of life.

[*Sound and movement of "seagull." Silence...* GUNSHOT.]

ARKADINA: [*Alarmed.*] What's that?

DORN: Nothing. Something in my medical bag probably exploded... Don't be alarmed.

ARKADINA: ...Oh, I got so frightened. I was reminded of when... [*Puts her hand over her face.*] I began to feel faint...

DORN: [*Lowers his voice.*] ...Take her away from here. The fact is Kostya shot himself.

[TRANSFORMATION.]

SONYA: We shall rest! We shall rest! We shall hear the angels; we shall see all Heaven lit with radiance; we shall see all earthly evil, all our sufferings, drowned in the mercy which will fill the whole world, and our life will be peaceful, gentle and sweet as a caress. I have faith, I have faith... we shall rest... we shall rest! We shall rest! We shall rest!

FIRS: Locked. They're gone.

[*Band* MUSIC, *faintly at first, building, then moving away again into the distance.*]

OLGA: The music plays so gaily, so valiantly, it makes you feel you want to live! Oh Dearest God! Time will pass, and we'll be gone forever — and we will be forgotten...

FIRS: They forgot about me.

OLGA: They will forget our faces, our voices, and even how many we were.

FIRS: Ah, well... it's nothing... I'll just sit here a bit...

OLGA: ... but our sufferings will turn to gladness for those who will live after us

FIRS: And he probably didn't put on his fur-coat, but went off in his top-coat... I didn't check...

OLGA: ... happiness and peace will come to earth, and people living then will be grateful to those who are living now.

FIRS: The young have so much to learn...

OLGA: Oh sweet sisters, our life is not yet ended. We shall live!

FIRS: Life has gone by, and it's as if I've never, ever lived.

OLGA: And the band plays so gaily, so valiantly, so joyfully...

FIRS: I'll lie down for just a little bit.

OLGA: In a moment, I feel, we will know why we live and why we suffer...

[*Band* MUSIC *fades out and is replaced by the dull thudding of an* AX.]

FIRS: You have no strength, have you...

OLGA: If only we could know!...

FIRS: Nothing remains...

OLGA: ...if only we could know!

FIRS: Nothing...

OLGA: If only we could know!...

FIRS: ...oh you...old fool...If only we could know...If only we could know...

[*Sound of the* AX *fades out.*]

[TRANSFORMATION.]

RANYEVSKAYA: Oh my sweet orchard, my dear and tender orchard, wonderful orchard!...My life, my youth, my happiness, Adieu...Farewell!...

FIRS: Oh you...old fool.

[*Silence. The* LIGHTS *come up on* OLGA KNIPPER.]

CODA

OLGA KNIPPER: "The theater, the theater! I don't know whether to love it or to curse it. Everything is so alluringly mixed up in this life! Now, except for the theater, I have nothing in my life." All those three years were a continuous struggle for me. I lived in a constant state of self-reproach. That's why I was so restless and erratic, couldn't settle down anywhere and make a home. As if I were acting against my conscience all the time. And yet, who knows — had I given up the stage..."

[*Long pause.*
  The LIGHTS *fade slowly to black.*]

END OF PLAY

PROPERTIES LIST

ACTRESS
Pince-nez
Earrings
hairclips
Watch
Shawl [*Arkadina*]
Cape [*Nina*]
Snuff box [*Masha*]
3 Aprons [*Sonya*]
Hat [*Dr. Chekhov*]
Large book
Pen
Blanket
Letter [*Olga Knipper*]
Fan [*Nina*]
2 Telegrams [*Ranyevskaya*]
Fur Hat [*Ranyevskaya*]
Fur Muff [*Ranyevskaya*]
Lace Collar [*Olga*]
Lace hat [*Maria Vasilyevna*]
Needlepoint
Purse w/make-up [*Arkadina*]
Cigarette holder [*Olga Knipper*]

ACTOR
Handkerchief
Watch
Ascot [*Trigorin*]
Hat [*Dorn*]
Pince-nez [*Dorn*]

Gun [*Vanya*]
Peasant Cap [*Medvedenko*]
Student cap [*Trofimov*]
Military cap [*Vershinin*]
Tin of fruit drops [*Gayev*]
Lapel flower [*Gayev*]
Doctor's Hat [*The Doctors*]
Pince-nez [*The Doctors*]
Sashe [*Andrey*]
Violin [*Andrey*]
Abacus [*Vanya*]
Account Book [*Vanya*]
Walking Stick [*Sorin*]
2 scarves [*Firs*]
Bandages [*Konstantin*]
Manuscripts
Wire-rim glasses [*Trofimov*]
Keys [*Lopakhin*]

SET PROPS

2 Cigarette boxes
2 Ashtrays
Glass of water
Empty champagne bottle
2 Quill pens
1 Inkwell
Brandy decanter
2 Snifters
Coffee cup and saucer
Wheelchair

Authors' Note On Transformation

The practice on the process of Transformation, which is a way of stepping from one character and circumstance to another, is a technique which Ms. Gans and Mr. Charney have learned and taught from the sixties to the nineties with great success. It is a method by which actors can create and perform numerous characters in a single evening; by finding the Imaginary Center, the Imaginary Body, the Psychological Gesture of each character, as well as the proper rhythm and mood for every scene, we were able to discover the inner life and artistic form for each of the thirty-four characters we were to portray.

As we moved from one scene to another, we were able to transform ourselves instantaneously into the imaginary Body of the next character, as if we were putting on a new costume or "stepping into the shoes" of the character who was there in all his immediacy, awaiting us with all his idiosyncrasies and unique character traits.

When we added a few simple props (apron, moustache, shawl, brandy snifter) the scenes seemed to unfold one after the other, each with its own peculiar atmosphere, time, place, rhythm, and Given Circumstances.

We believe this became possible because the entire galaxy of characters and scenes were our own previous creations, and like an imaginary film unfolding, they awaited the life that only the actor could give them. It was as if we stepped from one room into the next, from one world into another; and there the characters were waiting to claim us, to possess us. All we needed to do was surrender our life to them to become one with their creation.

We would like to stress that the unique magic of Transformation lies in the transition from scene to scene; from character to character, whereby the body of the character while making the gesture or movement transforms in the MIDDLE of his movement, into the gesture and voice (including rhythm, age, posture, etc.) of the next character, so that it is not the completion of one character and then the beginning of a new character, but rather one character rooted in and coming out of another character; like an old woman coming out of a young girl so that the intermediate process of Transformation takes place before your eyes without a break.

The same kind of Transformation is essential for one scene coming out of another according to the Given Circumstances (time, weather, the place, the Why, the Wish, the Obstacle), e.g. from a warm, dry, indoor fireplace to an outdoor bench on a bitter windy day.

One word more. It is the Psychological Gesture which leads to the heart and soul of the character. Finding the Psychological Gesture can take a long or short time — depending on the affinity the actor has with a particular character. Finding the precise psychology of the character is probably the most important and difficult task. It is, however, the swiftest way for the artist to create the seventeen different characters this work demands, as well as the profundity necessary in a play of this nature.

JORDAN CHARNEY is a noted actor, playwright, director, and teacher. Mr. Charney created the role of Al in the world premiere production of Steve Tesich's *On the Open Road*; appeared on Broadway in William Nicholson's *Shadowlands*, Lanford Wilson's *Talley's Folly*, Harold Pinter's *The Birthday Party*, Tennessee Williams' *Slapstick Tragedy*; Off-Broadway in the works of Albee, Pinter, Carlino, Beckett, etc.; regional theater appearances include Hartford Stage Co., Arena Stage in Washington, DC, South Coast Rep., the Goodman in Chicago, Yale Rep., and, most recently, the Huntington Theater in Boston, where he portrayed Claudius in the acclaimed production of *Hamlet* (Campbell Scott); television audiences enjoyed his many movie and series roles particularly his recurring role as Mr. Angelino on *Three's Company*; film credits include *Ghostbusters*, *Network*, *Hospital*, and *Plaza Suite*. He authored the book and lyrics for the critically acclaimed *The Sad Tale of King Leerio or Everyone Deserves a Second Chance*, a musical for children of all ages (music by Richard DeMone). Mr. Charney has served as Artistic Director for theater companies in Los Angeles, New York, and Boston, directing many prize-winning productions and creating several improvisational musical and comedy groups, and has developed the *STEPS System of Acting* which he teaches in New York and Los Angeles. He is currently preparing *The Throb of Life @ the Kindness of Strangers*, a screenplay for his Los Angeles STEPS Theater Company. The performing and "co-composing" of *A Chekhov Concert* was the realization of a dream.

SHARON GANS — As an actress, author, teacher, and director, Ms. Gans' unique talent and philosophy have influenced countless audiences around the world. She garnered the prestigious Obie Award as Best Actress in Sharon Thie's *Soon. Jack, November*, starred in the world premiere production of *Viet Rock*, *America Hurrah!*, and *Bechlch and Futz* (landmark theatrical productions of the sixties) in addition to haveing roles created for her by such playwrights as Megan Terry, Jean-Claude van Itallie, Rochelle Owens, Sam Shepard, and Alexander Francis Horn, to name a few. It was as an original member of the Open Theater (recipient of the Obie Award for four consecutive years), which she helped to co-found along with Joseph Chaikin, its primary director as well as Jean-Claude van Itallie and Peter Feldman, that Ms. Gans helped develop the technique of Transformation, which served as the process of presentation for *A Chekhov Concert*. Some of her favorite roles include Marguerite in Williams' *Camino Real*, Rebecca West in Ibsen's *Rosmersholm*, and the Courtesan in Buchner's *Danton's Death*. Film appearances include Peter Brook's *U.S.*, Michelangelo Antonioni's *Zabriskie Point*, and her starring role in George Roy Hill's *Slaughterhouse Five*. Ms. Gan's direction of over 30 major productions has been seen in London, Tel Aviv, Jerusalem, Munich, Berlin, Amsterdam, and the U.S. — most recently the critically acclaimed Off-Broadway U.S. premiere of the Howard Barker version of *Women Beware Women*. Ms. Gans is the author of the soon-to-be published *Leaping for the Rope or for Students Carrying the Work into the 21st Century*.

CHEKHOV:
THE MAJOR PLAYS

English versions by
Jean-Claude van Itallie

The Cherry Orchard
"A CLASSIC RESTORED TO THE HAND, MIND AND BLOOD OF THE CREATOR."
—*The New York Times*

The Seagull
"SUBLIMELY UNDERSTOOD CHEKHOV ...ABSOLUTELY TRUE TO THE ORIGINAL"
—*The New York Post*

Three Sisters
"CAPTURES CHEKHOV'S EXUBERANCE, MUSIC AND COMPLEXITY" —*The Village Voice*

Uncle Vanya
"THE CRISPEST AND MOST POWERFUL VERSION EXTANT." —*The New Republic*

Paper•ISBN 1-55783-162-9 • $7.95

APPLAUSE

GHOST IN THE MACHINE

A New Play
by David Gilman

"A devilishly clever puzzler of a comedy...it traps us in a web of uncertainty till we begin to wecond guess with the characters."
—Jan Stewart, *New York Newsday*

"A vastly entertaining whodunit, a chess game with human pieces that does not limit itself...Gilman teases us with philosophical questions on the nature of reality..."
—Laurie Winer, *The Los Angeles Times*

"Atight theatrical puzzle, the play echoes both the menacing personal relationships at the center of Harold Pinter's work and the complex mathematical equations that animate Tom Stoppard...but it is also very much of its own thing."
—Hedy Weiss, *The Chicago Sun Times*

Ghost in the the Machine begins with a common situation-that of a missing fifty dollar bill-and spins it into intriguing questions of probability, chance and the complexities of musical composition: illusion and reality.

Paper•ISBN 1-55783-228-5• $6.95
Performance rights available from APPLAUSE

APPLAUSE

The Day the Bronx Died

A Play
by Michael Henry Brown

"THE DAY THE BRONX DIED COMES ON LIKE GANGBUSTERS...LIKE A CAREENING SUBWAY TRAIN spewing its points in a series of breathless controntations"
—MICHAEL MUSTO, *The New York Daily News*

"Michael Henry Brown is A SMOKING VOLCANO OF A WRITER...THE DAY THE BRONX DIED is an engrossin drama... the danger exceeds our expectations"
—JAN STUART, *New York Newsday*

Two childhood friends—one black, the other white—struggle to live in a racist world.

Michael Henry Brown wrote the screenplay, DEAD PRESIDENTS directed by the Hughes brothers. He is the author of the HBO Mini-series LAUREL AVENUE. Among his other plays is GENERATION OF THE DEAD IN THE ABYSS OF CONEY ISLAND MADNESS which was produced to great acclaim at the Long Wharf Theatre in New Haven and the Penumbra Theatre in St. Paul

Paper•ISBN 1-55783-229-3 • $6.95
Performance rights available from APPLAUSE

APPLAUSE

MICHAEL CHEKHOV:
ON THEATER AND THE ART OF ACTING
The Six Hour Master Class
Four 90-minute Audio Cassettes
by Michael Chekhov

edited with a 48-page course guide
by Mala Powers

AN AUDIO TREASURE!

Join the legendary teacher/director, heralded as Russia's greatest actor, for a six hour master class on the fundamentals of the Chekhov technique. Among the features:

- The Art of Characterization
- Short Cuts to Role Preparation
- How to Awaken Artistic Feelings and Emotions
- Avoiding Monotony in Performance
- Overcoming Inhibitions and Building Self-Confidence
- Psycho-physical Exercises
- Development of the Ensemble Spirit

ISBN: 1-55783-117-3

APPLAUSE

THE BRUTE
& OTHER FARCES
BY ANTON CHEKHOV

edited by Eric Bentley

"INDISPENSABLE!"
—Robert Brustein, Director Loeb Drama Center
Harvard University

All the farces of Russia's greatest dramatist are rendered here in classic lively translations which audiences and scholars alike applaud on the stage and in the classroom. The blustering, stuttering eloquence of Chekhov's unlikely heroes has endured to shape the voice of contemporary theatre. This volume presents seven minor masterpieces:

THE HARMFULNESS OF TOBACCO
SWAN SONG
A MARRIAGE PROPOSAL
THE CELEBRATION
A WEDDING
SUMMER IN THE COUNTRY
THE BRUTE

ISBN: 1-55783-004-5

APPLAUSE